CONTEN

Poetry Book Society

Poetry Book Society Memberships

Choice

4 Books a Year: 4 Choice books & 4 *Bulletins* (UK £55, Europe £65, ROW £75)

World

8 Books: 4 Choices, 4 Translation books & 4 *Bulletins* (£98, £120, £132)

Charter

20 Books: 4 Choices, 16 Recommendations & 4 *Bulletins* (£180, £210, £235)

Complete

24 Books: 4 Choices, 16 Recommendations, 4 Translations & 4 *Bulletins* (£223, £265, £292)

Single copies of the *Bulletin* £9.99

Cover Art *I Want To Live With No Fear,* courtesy of Shilpa Gupta **Photographer** Scott Beseler

ISBN 9781913129279 ISSN 0551-1690

Poetry Book Society | Milburn House | Dean Street | Newcastle upon Tyne | NE1 1LF

0191 230 8100 | enquiries@poetrybooksociety.co.uk

WWW.POETRYBOOKS.CO.UK

LETTER FROM THE PBS

This Autumn *Bulletin* will be shipping as summer ends. I hope you have all managed to have a break and enjoy some of the good weather we have had, whether home or abroad – maybe even been to a literary event or two! And we thank you for making the choice to buy from the PBS, buying fabulous poetry books direct from us over the summer and into autumn. We know there are other options out there and we really appreciate your support!

The Autumn Choice goes to Hannah Lowe with *The Kids*. She writes in her commentary that she learnt as much as she taught in her time as a secondary school teacher; such a beautiful sentiment which feels apt for the selections in this *Bulletin*. You can watch Hannah reading her poems online at our PBS Showcase with Kazim Ali and Nidhi Zak/Aria Eipe at Durham Book Festival in October and at a virtual PBS NCLA event with Raymond Antrobus at 7pm on the 25th November. Check out our website and social media for details.

Across this brilliant array of titles there is an invitation to pause for thought and to learn. We are asked to question how to live in the world today, read the space and the silence, consider the climate emergency, parenthood, untethered bodies, internationalism. There is so much to absorb, appreciate and take in from the collections, personally I am finding it hard to decide where to begin.

We are always looking for ways to support poets and their writing, and we now have resources to help you, our readers, with your reading! Introducing Readers Notes, which will be available in the Members Area of our website as soon as this *Bulletin* has taken flight. Three poems are included from this season's titles with helpful discussion points. We hope this will be useful for those of you in poetry book clubs, and those reading independently. Alongside our Instagram Live Book Club, which you can catch up with on our Youtube channel, we are creating a brilliant PBS member's resource.

Prize season will be upon us before we know it, as with previous years we have a special "bundle" offer for the Forward Prizes including all ten shortlisted titles, available to order from our website www.poetrybooks.co.uk or over the phone.

SOPHIE O'NEILL
PBS & INPRESS DIRECTOR

Image: Lealle Bissessar

HANNAH LOWE

Hannah Lowe was born in Ilford to an English mother and Jamaican-Chinese father. She has worked as a teacher of literature, and is now a lecturer in Creative Writing at Brunel University. Her first book-length collection *Chick* (Bloodaxe Books, 2013) won the Michael Murphy Memorial Prize, was shortlisted for the Forward Prize for Best First Collection, the Fenton Aldeburgh First Collection Prize, the Seamus Heaney Centre Prize for Poetry, and was selected for the Poetry Book Society's Next Generation Poets 2014 promotion. This was followed by her family memoir *Long Time No See* (Periscope, 2015), which was a BBC Radio 4 Book of the Week. Her second collection *Chan* was published by Bloodaxe Books in 2016 and in 2020 she received a Cholmondeley Award from the Society of Authors.

THE KIDS

BLOODAXE BOOKS | £10.99 | PBS PRICE £8.25

The opening of the very first poem in this collection of sonnets sets up the tension and rhythm within the confines of the form which Lowe is able to make great use of:

My father was dead. I rode to work each morning
through Farringdon, down Charterhouse Street,
and saw the same white dog – a terrier – licking
a puddle of blood, leaked by the morning meat

The play of caesura against enjambement, the cleverness of the ending of line three, which presents something cute before giving us immediate and visceral horror as we turn into the next line, show Lowe fully at home, calm and confident as a sonneteer.

Lowe has spoken elsewhere of the idea of the sonnet as a classroom, which makes me think both of its walls of containment and its windows outside. The other layer here is the awareness of sonnet traditions within education: early on the poet climbs past "Shakespeare's doubtful face" on the way to teach, and in 'The Art of Teaching II', we are told that:

> Boredom hangs like a low cloud in the classroom...
> ...there is no volta here, no turn,
> just more of the same

The language of the sonnet itself becomes the language of the environment, just as the classroom itself mimics that sonnet shape.

As the collection progresses, we move backwards from the teacher to the pupil, exploring the awkward triumphs and difficulties of adolescence, and then forwards into motherhood, and the raising of a child. Sometimes the sonnet unrolls its lines, sometimes it tips sideways and, at one vital moment, in 'The Stroke', five sonnets run together, the emotion and weight of the moment temporarily breaking down the form's own defences.

Always, we are in the hands of Lowe's singular, effortless voice, and reminded that all good education should be an education in class, in the legacies and history of empire and in the self.

ANDREW McMILLAN

HANNAH LOWE

I wanted to pay homage to the teenagers I taught over years at a sixth form college in London. Looking back, I saw how much I'd learnt from them. They indelibly affected my thinking about all kinds of things – race, social class, gender, language, culture. I think the experience of teaching is always also the experience of learning.

The poems move between my life as a teacher and as a learner. I sometimes use the "turn" in the sonnet to make that shift. I was profoundly affected by my own experience of education at their age. After attending a very traditional school, I was lucky to be taught by a teacher called John Toolan at FE college in Essex. He delivered a very radical literary curriculum which galvanised my love of reading. The book is dedicated to him.

The sonnet seemed the perfect form, initially because of its associations with education, Shakespeare, high culture. I wanted to expand its parameters to write about working class experiences, slang, subcultures. Of course, I'm not the first poet to push the boundaries of the sonnet. I was influenced by many other sonnet writers, both traditional and experimental.

My son, Rory, is both the student and teacher of the later sequence, and my father stands behind these poems. I think he'll always be a catalyst to my writing. I became a teacher because I needed to find purpose in my life after his death. My mother is there too. She was a primary school teacher for over thirty years.

I also wanted to write about the other kinds of education, and express my gratitude to those who have taught me about poetry. Many people helped me write this book, so the collection is also a testament to my own learning about the sonnet and its possibilities.

HANNAH RECOMMENDS

Jeff Hilson, *The Reality Street Book of Sonnets* (Reality Street); Phillis Levin (ed.), *The Penguin Book of the Sonnet: One Hundred Years of a Classic Tradition*; Moira Egan, *Bar Napkin Sonnets* (The Ledge Press); Jacqueline Saphra, *One Hundred Lockdown Sonnets* (Nine Arches Press); Anna Selby, *Field Notes* (Hazel Press); Vicki Morris, *If All This Never Happened* (Southword Editions); Mimi Khalvati, *Afterwardness* (Carcanet); Richard Price, *The Owner of the Sea: Three Inuit Stories Retold* (Carcanet); Philip Levine, *Stranger to Nothing* (Bloodaxe Books); Marie Howe, *What the Living Do* (W.W. Norton).

THE ONLY ENGLISH KID

When the debate got going on "Englishness",
I'd pity the only English kid – poor Johnny
in his spotless Reeboks and blue Fred Perry.
He had a voice from history: *Dunno-miss,*
Yes-miss, No-miss – all treacly-cockney,
rag-and-bone – and while the others claimed Poland,
Ghana, Bulgaria, and shook off England
like the wrong team's shirt, John brewed his tea

exclusively on Holloway Road. So when Aasif
mourned the George Cross banner swinging freely
like a warning from his neighbour's roof,
the subway tunnel sprayed with MUSLIM SCUM,
poor John would sit there quietly, looking guilty
for all the awful things he hadn't done.

BALLOONS

These five-year-olds remind me of the balloons
we had one summer: heart-shaped helium,
in rainbow colours; we pushed notes inside them
and let them go, believing that the moon
might catch those small hearts climbing up the sky.
I watch these children knelt around their teacher,
their small hands shooting high to give an answer,
any answer, just the chance to try.

But the kids I taught, who came to me at the edge
of childhood – was it really, then, too late?
In the common room we said it only took
one class, one hour, to know the grades they'd get,
as though there were a Magic 8 Ball, wedged
at one conclusion, no matter how hard you shook.

RAYMOND ANTROBUS

Raymond Antrobus was born in Hackney, London, to an English mother and Jamaican father, he is the author of *To Sweeten Bitter* and *The Perseverance*. In 2019 he became the first ever poet to be awarded the Rathbone Folio Prize for the best work of literature in any genre. Other accolades include the Ted Hughes Award, PBS Winter Choice, a *Sunday Times* Young Writer of the Year Award and *The Guardian* Poetry Book Of The Year 2018, as well as being shortlisted for the Griffin and Forward Prizes. In 2018 he was awarded The Geoffrey Dearmer Prize, judged by Ocean Vuong, for his poem 'Sound Machine'. His poem 'Jamaican British' was added to the GCSE syllabus in 2019.

ALL THE NAMES GIVEN

PICADOR | £10.99 | PBS PRICE £8.25

The follow-up to Antrobus' multi-award winning debut begins with a poem of thanks ("Give thanks to the wheels touching tarmac at JFK") which deftly lands the reader into the collection. This is a book which feels as though it is searching for different ways to connect; never more so than the dead and the living – be that geographically, emotionally, through spoken words, through sign language, or even through innovative soundscape notation: "[sound of connection across time"]. These poems too are interested in the stories we tell of ourselves, and the way we learn of other people through them.

In 'Text and Image', the poet considers long distance love, "how can I show you // my love is unfolding if my words / can't reach you glowing and wild"; 'Text and Image' recurs later on, the poem reformed into a surreal dream. Again that desire to fully connect, and the search for how that might be achieved. As the collection continues, the caption poems which have occupied their own single space begin to interject between the lines of poems; bringing together the two forms into an important formal innovation. This makes poems like 'The Royal Opera House (with stage captions)' and 'Horror Scene as Black English Royal (captioned)' three-dimensional and lifts them off the page. The final poem, in this layered and immensely moving collection, seems to speak to the book's whole project:

I lose my hearing aids
and move more fluid

the same way I do
when I swim the way
I do when I sex

the thing
the neighbours hear

through the walls
is me being pushed
out of myself

It's silence that stills
the noise in my eyes.

Reader, this is the place
I try to take you
when I close them.

ANDREW McMILLAN

RAYMOND ANTROBUS

Silence is often thought about as something passive but this book, *All The Names Given,* is an immersive poetry collection that attempts to engage and activate silences and the "white space" that surrounds them on the page. In some ways it picks up from where *The Perseverance* left off, thinking about sound, miscommunication, education, history, place and memory that is at once personal and public (loud and quiet) but in other ways it explores new territory as the poems meditate on marriage, intimacy and the speaker's English mother. The book takes wide-ranging inspiration from the Deaf sound artist Christine Sun Kim to the 19th century Spanish poet Juan Ramón Jiménez.

I'm finding it difficult to sum up everything that I attempt to explore in the book, it is very much a further "investigation of missing sounds", but I like something that Don Paterson said: "Throughout, *All The Names Given* is punctuated with [Caption Poems] which attempt to fill in the silences and transitions between the poems, as well as moments inside and outside of them. Direct, open, formally sophisticated, *All The Names Given* breaks new ground both in form and content: the result is a timely, humane and tender book".

[unstoppable singing]

and this is where everyone in the Royal Opera House, Black,
white, whatever, rises to their feet and shouts and hollers and
claps and cries and none of the silences, none of them are filled.

- Extract from 'The Royal Opera House (with Stage Captions)'

RAYMOND RECOMMENDS

Some poetry books I have read recently that I enjoyed are Adam Zagajewski, *Canvas* (FSG); Kazim Ali, *The Voice of Sheila Chandra* (Platypus Press); Tishani Doshi, *A God At The Door* (Bloodaxe Books); Gerald Stern, *Odd Mercy* (W.W. Norton); Gboyega Odubanjo, *Aunty Uncle Poems* (Poetry Business); Gail McConnell, *The Sun Is Open* (Penned in the Margins); Kayo Chingonyi, *A Blood Condition* (Chatto & Windus).

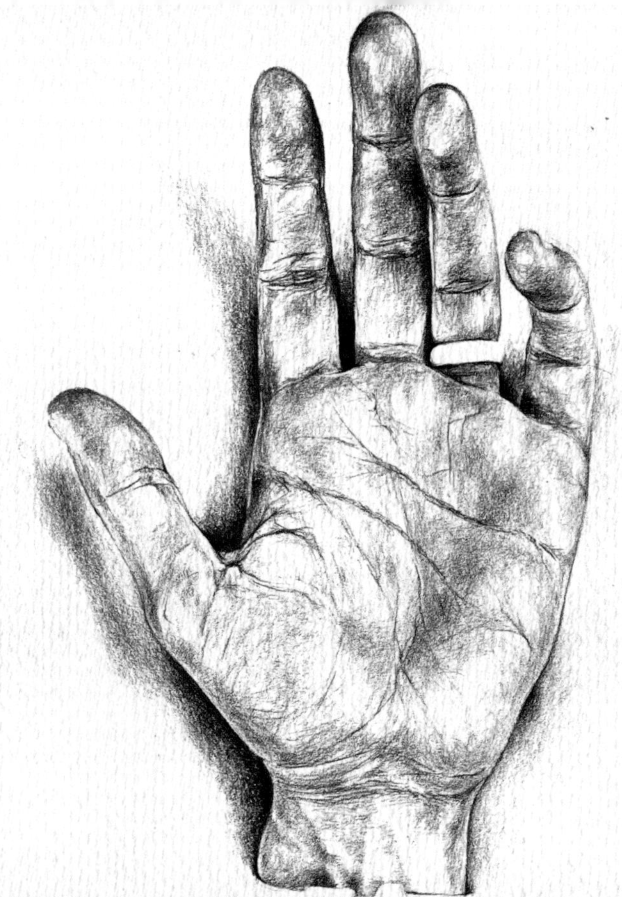

Here, take my pulse, take my breath,

take my arms as I drift off

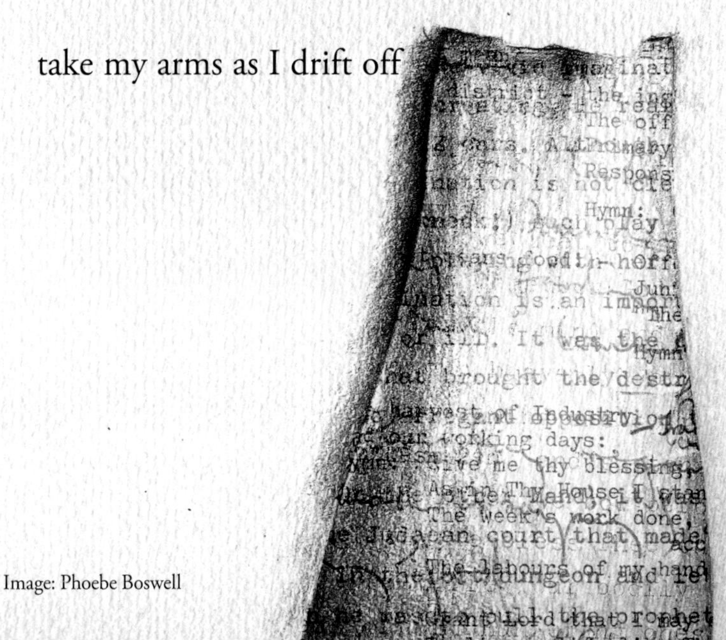

Image: Phoebe Boswell

TEXT AND IMAGE

Tabitha; *Dreamt I was in my studio,*
conserving this painting, slowly sharpening scalpels.

I'm neat and focused until my fingernails
became a large feeling that the painting couldn't understand me.

Meanwhile my fingernails start scratching the canvas,
I lose it and hold the painting, tearing the whole thing in half.

Then there are twelve more paintings at my feet
(Warhol's, Marclay's, Hockney's) and I'm picking up each

and tearing and tearing until my finger nails fell off, became swords
and all the paintings became my uncle (who was murdered)

but there was no blood on his body, just bright blue
and yellow paint and someone kept saying

master, master, master, master, master.

TOGARA MUZANENHAMO

Togara Muzanenhamo was born in Zambia and brought up in Zimbabwe. He has studied in France, the Netherlands, and the United Kingdom. His poems have appeared widely in international journals and magazines. His debut poetry collection *Spirit Brides* (Carcanet, 2006) was shortlisted for the Jerwood Aldeburgh First Collection Prize and his second book *Gumiguru* (Carcanet, 2014) was shortlisted for the Glenna Luschei Prize for African Poetry.

VIRGA

CARCANET PRESS | £10.99 | PBS PRICE £8.25

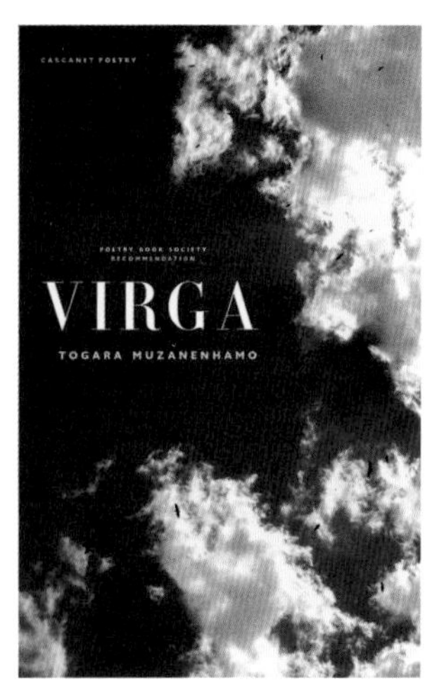

Togara Muzanenhamo's *Virga* is named for a meteorological phenomenon in which rain falls, visible in the sky as dark shafts or streaks below the clouds, but then evaporates before it can hit the earth. The resulting downdrafts can crash planes. It becomes a metaphor in the book for lives suspended, purposes that miss their mark, sudden turbulence. Muzanenhamo is one of Zimbabwe's most prominent contemporary English-language poets. There are poems in *Virga* that continue his earlier work's interest in Africa's colonial and postcolonial past, set on a global stage. The book opens with 'Swakopmund', a long poem that takes us into the mind of a German setting sail from the Namibian port with a hold full of "conscripts" for the Kaiser's genocidal African campaigns. The echoes of earlier phases of slavery are unavoidable:

> He can not cleanse his mind
> of the men staggering shackled
> over the knurled wash of the mole.

Just as the weather doesn't observe the boundaries of nations, *Virga's* imagination is restlessly cosmopolitan. Containing poems set across different cultures and decades of the twentieth century, it holds up to the light half-forgotten figures from history, and indeed expands our sense of history. Framed in a close third-person, or occasionally as monologues, the poems imagine pivotal moments in the lives of an eclectic cast of characters, from the Japanese polar explorer Terutaro Takeda who followed in the wake of Captain Scott, to the German chess champion Emanuel Lasker, to the French athlete and concert pianist, Micheline Ostermeyer, among many others. We see Ostermeyer throw her medal-winning shot at the 1948 Olympics, suspended mid-air – like virga – at the poem's end:

> A note hanging briefly.
> Waiting.
> To hit the earth.

The effect is reminiscent of the orchestral quality of David Mitchell's early novels, as we meet an array of fascinating people under a "sky that quickly saturates with every colour of faith".

SARAH HOWE

TOGARA MUZANENHAMO

From strange white clouds decimating whole villages in northern Cameroon in 1986, to the spiritual silence of a sundog on the edge of an ice-field during the 1911 Japanese Antarctic Expedition, to the 1921 World Championship chess matches in the Cuban heat, or the final hours of a young Bavarian mountaineer suspended beneath a rock ledge in the Bernese Alps in 1936 – *Virga* draws its inspiration from various historical events set in the twentieth century, the poems interwoven by the weather and the wind.

The project began over a decade ago after I came across a book of powerful photographs, *Century: One Hundred Years of Human Progress, Regression, Suffering and Hope*, edited by the British writer and photographer Bruce Bernard. *Century* cast an eye on what Bernard described as, "the most thoughtless, but in other ways the most thoughtful, hundred years in human history... offering nothing to provide us with any firm grounds for either bright hope or black despair." As I worked through my second book, *Gumiguru*, the photographs in *Century* had infiltrated my subconscious so greatly that I found myself collecting and sketching ideas from factual events from the 1900s – but unlike the broad retrospect of Bernard's photographic compendium – I was more interested in stories off the mainstream historical path, of lesser known events.

Initially, the common thread of the collection was the timeline of the twentieth century, but as I worked on the poems I began to realise that over the one hundred years that defined the twentieth century – the weather has changed more dramatically than in any other time in modern history. It was with this thought in mind that I decided to use the weather as the backdrop of the collection – and in some cases the weather may also be seen as a character through stories of war, music, phenomena of nature, philately, sport, dance forms and even ufology – the poems capture stories told through a fast evolving century encased beneath an ancient, fragile sky.

TOGARA RECOMMENDS

Franca Mancinelli, *The Little Book of Passage* (Bitter Oleander); Robin Robertson, *The Long Take* (Picador); Kerstin Ekman, *The Dog* (Sphere); Martinus Nijhoff, *Awater* (Anvil); Cormac McCarthy, *The Crossing* (Picador); Don Mee Choi, *DMZ Colony* (Wave); Batsirai Chigama, *Gather the Children* (Ntombekhaya); Sharmistha Mohanty, *The Gods Came Afterwards* (Speaking Tiger); Carolyn Forché, *In the Lateness of the World* (Bloodaxe); James Davies, *Stack* (Carcanet Press); Tracy K. Smith, *Wade in the Water* (Graywolf); Raul Zurita, *Sky Below: Selected Works* (Curbstone); Gerður Kristný, *Reykjavik Requiem* (Arc).

Image: © CarIN / Alamy

VIRGA

"Se dirá que tenemos
en uno de los ojos mucha pena
y también en el otro, mucha pena
y en los dos, cuando miran, mucha pena..."
– César Vallejo

Must have been the thunder
rolling down the mountainside that made the clown
lead the children to higher ground –
the circus tent left behind
with all its theatre – then swallowed whole three minutes later.
Fifty years on you can still see
four half buried palm trees.
Fragments of the cathedral wall beside the old cemetery.
A wrecked bus raised like a strange crustacean riding a wave of rock.
Hard to imagine how it all came down.
The black rush off Huascarán's shoulder. Mud. Ice. Boulders.
Everything sealed beneath the earth.
A statue of Christ with open arms stares down from the old cemetery's hill.
From the high ground – three hundred children
had watched the highland town erased with all they'd known.
The dead never exhumed.
Only names floating dark with grief.
The veiled altocumulus above our heads –
drifting
and thinning out
over Callejón de Huaylas.

JACK UNDERWOOD

Jack Underwood's debut collection of poems *Happiness* (Faber, 2015) won the Somerset Maugham Award. He is a Senior Lecturer in English and Creative Writing at Goldsmiths College, University of London. His non-fiction book *Not Even This*, about parenthood, uncertainty, poetic language and knowledge, was published by Corsair.

A YEAR IN THE NEW LIFE

FABER | £10.99 | PBS PRICE £8.25

Readers of Jack Underwood's debut collection, *Happiness*, might recall these lines from 'William', a lovely little poem of awe and fear at holding a newborn: "I can feel my socks being on – / utter, precious apple, / churchyards flatten in my heart, / I've never been brilliant so scared." One or two such notes retrospectively point the way towards *A Year in the New Life*, which brings a fresh intensity of feeling to the original and off-kilter vision for which Underwood is known.

In this second book, he puts his distinctive stamp on what Stephanie Burt has called "The New Poetry of New Fatherhood", explored on this side of the Atlantic by poets from Robert Crawford to Caleb Klaces. Fathering becomes a route into uncovering the gentler side of more traditional masculinities: "I've never wanted to fight anyone / ever, or be real this way and mean it. / I just want to bellow love unbridled" ('I am become a man'). The new father's runaway anxiety and floored tenderness are two recurring threads. Love in these poems is an ecstatic spilling over:

> How much love do I have inside me now?
> As in the effect of mass on the curvature
> of space-time, or? OK, OK, something
> you can see. Maybe
>
> rapeseed yellow,
> every day,
> the whole fucking field.

On display still is Underwood's habit of self-consciously tinkering with the mechanics of metaphor-making, whose descent into something automatic ("pigeon-pewter or urinal-cake sky, whatever") is parodied elsewhere. The collection spirals away into broader anxieties about the right way to live in the world, about societal and environmental collapse. But since this is Jack Underwood – I quietly chuckled my way through many of these poems – he can't help holding up those big themes ("a bite taken out / of the grand old narrative") as if between tweezers, quizzically:

> Deep time. Homely time.
> The human print will not survive.
> I mean like, woo, there it was.

SARAH HOWE

JACK UNDERWOOD

I find it very difficult to write about my poems in prose; it feels like hosing them down in a courtyard. This is because it seems to me that a poem is about its subject in the same kind of way that a person might be said to dance about the room, or a tree be about ten metres high, and I so struggle to know what it is I am writing about before I can even figure out what I want to write about it. These feelings or inclinations are complicated further by the fact that *A Year in the New Life* was written over a period of seven years, during which time I became a father.

I had been researching and writing a non-fiction book about uncertainty, in particular how poems offer us a respite from the burden of reason, of always having to know, how they call us home to uncertainty, as a positive cognitive stance, even though such a stance might situate us in various positions of vulnerability. My daughter arrived in a human world tangibly and irrecoverably malfunctioning, and her vulnerability terrified me. I found myself resituated in it, or in relation to it, in ways I could not control or comprehend.

Outside, it got worse and worse and every so often I wrote a poem: a poem about fear, a poem about gratitude, a poem about love, about joy, about her, about me, about difficulty, love again, fear again, and sometimes many of these things at once.

I'm filled / with the fear
of the joy / no the sadness
of the joy / a leaf
on a street / what I mean
if you don't know / what I mean
by the sadness / of the joy
is forgive me / I mean don't worry

JACK RECOMMENDS

A few books I have enjoyed recently include Natalie Shapero, *Popular Longing* (Copper Canyon Press); Joyelle McSweeney, *Toxicon and Arachne* (Nightboat Books); Sara Peters, *I Become a Delight to My Enemies* (Strange Light); Kaveh Akbar, *Pilgrim Bell* (Graywolf Press); Rachel Long, *My Darling From the Lions* (Picador); Dom Hale, *Scammer* (The 87 Press); Holly Pester, *Comic Timing* (Granta Books); Luke Kennard, *Notes on the Sonnets* (Penned in the Margins) and Peter Gizzi, *Sky Burial* (Carcanet Press).

MY NAME IS ZONAL COORDINATOR

Listen to my voice happening inside you.
Feel the way I pronounce these words,
moving them through you like fruits
of different sizes and shapes. *Apricot.*
I'm going to move the word *apricot*
to touch against your liver. Is that OK?
Do you know where your liver is?
Apricot. There, you've found it.
You are beginning to feel lighter.
You are on a generic tropical beach.
Your wisdom teeth are calm and happy.
Your family forgives you. You are lava
rising through the mantle of the world
oblivious to events upon its surface.
Your friends like you. You are floating.
My peregrine will guide you.
See small adjustments to her wing-tips.
Nothing is holding you up now.
The second digit of your security number
has fallen far away. No one is cross
with you. The world will return
to its natural state of non-existence,
but only when you do. Repeat after me:
I am feeling so good about myself.
I am feeling so good about myself.

A GIRL OR WOMAN IN RELATION TO EITHER OR BOTH OF HER PARENTS

also *noun* meaning weather as in I expect the good
daughter won't last or the daughter is expected to improve
at the weekend also *verb* meaning to be suddenly aware
of one's overwhelmedness as in we were daughtered
by the magnitude of the cave system also *adj* meaning
robust as in such behaviour was met with a daughter
response also *noun* meaning overseer as in a daughter
was assigned by the company to assess whose work
had been completed satisfactorily also *noun* meaning
metal jug for outdoor use as in we arrived at the shed
and the daughter was already full of autumn leaves
also *noun* meaning a situation that forces the mind
to conceive of the impossible as in suddenly we had
a daughter and it began to rain indoors.

Image: Angela Isaac Panat

NIDHI ZAK /ARIA EIPE

Nidhi Zak/Aria Eipe is a poet, pacifist and fabulist. Born in India, she grew up across the Middle East, Europe and North America, before calling Ireland home. She is poetry editor at Skein Press and Fallow Media, and contributing editor with *The Stinging Fly*. The recipient of a Next Generation Artist Award from the Arts Council of Ireland and the inaugural Ireland Chair of Poetry Student Award, she serves on the advisory board of Diversifying Irish Poetry in collaboration with Poetry Ireland and Ledbury Emerging Poetry Critics. *Auguries of a Minor God* (Faber, 2021) is her first collection.

AUGURIES OF A MINOR GOD

FABER | £10.99 | PBS PRICE £8.25

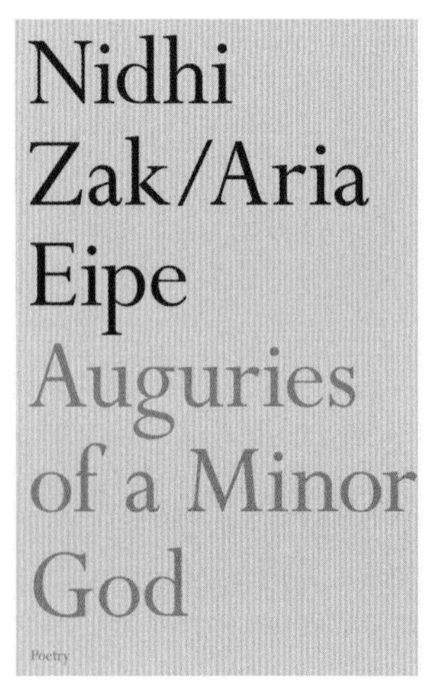

Nidhi Zak/Aria Eipe's debut collection is a book of two parts, linked by their enquiry into love, loss and the lingering traumas that can follow from migration. *Auguries of a Minor God* combines formal and typographical experimentation, such as the virgules that fracture these lines, with an unexpectedly plainspoken surface:

ammachi taught me how to kiss / my small face in her hands / cheekblade whetting mine / breathing in sharp / lungfilled as if / she had just been born / and I / so close / enough to smell / giddy heat / oiled ringlets / like coconut / like matriarch / tough brown outside / tender white inside / so

later / when he put his tongue / down my throat / I gave it back / because a man / who doesn't know / how to kiss you / doesn't deserve to / touch your hair

Nidhi Zak/Aria Eipe calls on a range of devices from the concrete poet's toolkit: irregular letter-spacing, words jammed together into breathless compounds, text arranged into visual patterns and greyed or crossed out. While playful, these manipulations also convey the broken motion of thoughts skewed by past suffering. The book's first part consists of short poems offering elliptical parables of love and cultural dislocation reminiscent, in flashes, of a poet like Warsan Shire. Its poems are divided into five sections, each named for the five arrows of Kāma, the Hindu God of Love, Desire and Memory.

The collection's second part reprises these enquiries in a different key: of Kāma's attributes, memory now comes to the fore. A long, onward-rushing narrative poem, 'A is for العرب (Arabs)', charts the efforts of a refugee family who have fled from an unnamed Middle Eastern country to settle in the West. Framed as an abecedarian, it is part story, part litany, part found poem:

> ...the
> heaviness of everything you've been holding in, the heartache and the sheer hopelessness, it all gets thrown together with the mundane stuff like the harissa and the hummus and the sadseeminglettuce...

You can start to see in this extract from "h" the poem's collision of cultures and tonalities, poised discomfortingly – as much of Nidhi Zak/Aria Eipe's work is – between levity and tragedy, between "heartache" and "mundane stuff".

SARAH HOWE

NIDHI ZAK/ARIA EIPE

"Only a god's word has no beginning or end. Only a god's desire can reach without lack. Only the paradoxical god of desire, exception to all these rules, is neverendingly filled with lack itself." – Anne Carson

Years ago, I was gifted a slim skyblue book. It was of unusual dimensions, wider than a book would usually be, a bespoke size harbouring a whole world. Kālidāsa's *Kumārasambhava*, in a majestic translation by Hank Heifetz: *The Origin of the Young God*. Kālidāsa has ever enchanted me lyrically in a way that no one else can, yet it was a minor character in this mahākāvya who completely captivated my heart. Kāma, the god of desire – a mere servant to the thirty three supreme deities of the Hindu pantheon – is tasked with seducing Shiva, the ultimate ascetic, into a moment of intimacy in which he will bear a child with Pārvati, birthing Kumāra – the young god – destined to be the vanquisher of demons and saviour of the gods.

What I loved Kālidāsa's Kāma for was his radiant frailty. His incendiary devotion. His divine failings. Kāma, the boy with the sugarcane bow, who proved the most vulnerable to the wounds that love makes. By the middle of the book, the fourth sarga, Kāma has been burned to ashes becoming "ananga" – one without a body – and the universe reels with loss.

Years later, when my mother died, in the sudden absence of this embodied sense of love, I was returned to the story of Kāma. What happens to the body when it comes untethered, through accident, death or transcendence? What happens to the body when it is touched, moved, stunned, displaced, disturbed, troubled, threatened, transformed, surprised, violated, intoxicated, awakened, liberated? These poems exist as invitations into the rapture and peril of this intimacy.

NIDHI RECOMMENDS

Kaveh Akbar, *Pilgrim Bell* (Graywolf Press); Threa Almontaser, *The Wild Fox of Yemen* (Picador); Supriya Kaur Dhaliwal, *The Yak Dilemma* (Makina Books); Benjamin Garcia, *Thrown in the Throat* (Milkweed); Seán Hewitt, *Tongues of Fire* (Cape); Ash Davida Jane, *How to Live with Mammals* (Victoria University Press); Charles Lang, *Aye ok* (Speculative Books); Ae Hee Lee, *Dear Bear,* (Platypus Press); Mícheál McCann, *Safe Home* (Green Bottle Press); Joyelle McSweeney, *Toxicon and Arachne* (Nightboat Books); Alycia Pirmohamed, *Hinge* (Ignition Press); Robin Robertson, *Grimoire* (Picador).

A IS FOR العرب (ARABS)

and they used not to wish each other joy but for three things: the

birth of a blessed babyblue boy, the foaling of a
beautiful broadboned mare, and the

coming to light of a promising poet,
conjuring his craft in the hallowed halls and
courts of princely benefactors, though these

days, Arabs are more likely to be
depicted as tyrants and terrorists, deprived of their
dignity in demeaning stripsearches, delineated as
dogs, detained naked under blackcloaks, blindfolds,
draped over with darkhoods at Abu Ghraib, so eager to

end their lives in the echo of jihad for the promise of
enchanting slimhipped houri in heaven, so that
even the rest of us – who should know better – tend to believe
extraordinary things about these people simply trying to
exist in a hostile world, and wasn't it an Arab, Ibrahim, who famously
extended his hospitality to the angels masquerading as messengers, who
entered his tent unasked, and didn't he bathe their hands, their feet,
encourage them to eat, offer those three strangers a bed for the night,

fetch only the finest food that he could find, slaughter his
fattest, plumppinched calf just so his guests could
feast on the tenderroast flesh, feed their brownskinnedbellies
full, for perhaps he understood what it felt like to be
foreign, to be flung far from the familiar, to live in
frequent fear for your life, for those you love, to ferry
five children across the fiercefoaming sea, to
find yourself having to choose between home and
family, to flee like fugitives until you hit another

fence, to face – unflinchingly – the unassailable
fact that from here on out, so much will be
forgotten: language, flavour, fragrance – so
fragile, this freedom you fight for; so

go now, get a house in the suburbs, white fence, white neighbours, watch them
glare at you from behind their gauzy diaphanous drapes while you wheel out the
green bin, turn up their noses as if you embody the stench that you simply carry;
get your kids ready for school, gobbling down their generic milkflake breakfasts,
gathering up your collective courage, waiting for the traffic lights to turn:
green says go, you're teaching them to chant, *red says stop, yellow*
get ready, green says go, but colour means other to you, means
green card, black list, pentahued pentagon terror levels, that's what's
going through your head later as you help them with homework, to get better
grades, try to grow them up well – because you need to teach them to be
good citizens but they are only children so it's futile – they simply don't
get it: that they are not citizen, not permanent, not resident, not anything, yet
giving up when you've got this far is not an option, even on the days when
grief drags you under like a body, sunk and heavy, not a vibrant one, not a
gentle animate thing, moving, spirited beside your own, like a river, like
grace, like your wife's face the last time you saw her, alive, radiant, the
glow of youth like rosehip, like pomegranate, like sumacscatteredfreckles,
glistening on her cheeks, in her hearthauntingeyes, what you wouldn't
give now for the glittering throat of her laughter, rolling out your rug,
genuflecting in the direction of your holy stone, calling out to the glory of your
god when all you have is her name in your mouth, perfectprayerbead on your tongue;

how you miss her now, on these days when it is so unendurably
hot and summer creeps down the insides of your arms like
handheld icecream on a woodentonguestick, and you force yourself to
head out to get some comfort food for the kids who will be only too
happy to stage a mini-mutiny if they are made to eat macaroni again, so,
heaving yourself off the sofa, you make your way across the block to that Syrian
hole in the wall, kept afloat by the old guy with the stinking sweetstalebreath –
Hamza, is that his name? – who always tells you the same bloody story: the
history of the desertdwelling Middle Eastern Bedouin Arabian
horses, how Our Prophet Muhammad released his thunderous
herd to race through the sands in search of water, after a long and arduous
haul through the desert, but after they had bolted, all at once...

KATE SIMPSON

Kate Simpson is an editor, author, poet and critic based in York. She is Associate Editor for *Aesthetica* Magazine, also working across Aesthetica's awards and events including the Aesthetica Art Prize, Creative Writing Award, BAFTA-Qualifying Film Festival and Future Now Symposium. Kate's critical and creative work has been published with *The London Magazine, Poetry Review*, The Poetry School and *Mslexia*, amongst others. In 2020, Kate joined Valley Press as Editor at Large. *Out of Time* is her first book, and is published in a seminal year for the environment, as the United Nations meet to accelerate action towards climate change.

OUT OF TIME: ED. KATE SIMPSON

VALLEY PRESS | £12.99 | PBS PRICE £9.75

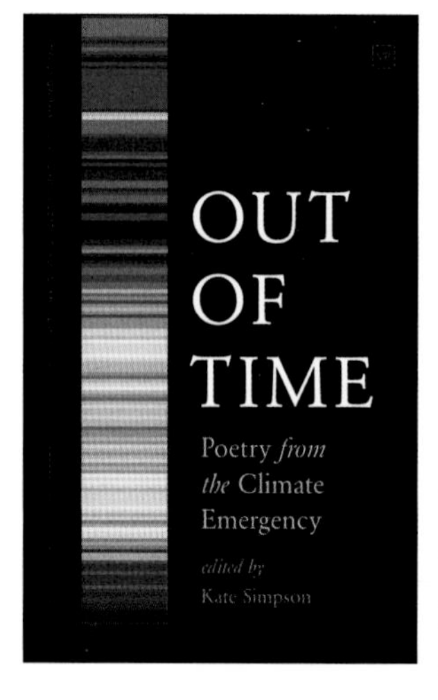

I remember a few years ago remarking to someone about the surprising absence of the climate emergency in contemporary poetry; the most pressing and immediate concern of our age seemed oddly absent – perhaps because poetry sometimes needs time to recollect in tranquillity before committing something to the page (and there is little chance of any tranquil time in the coming years) or perhaps we are too "in" the midst of it, too involved to be able to have that distance great poetry often requires.

This has been changing quickly in the last few years though, and the latest addition to the growing canon is this anthology, edited by Kate Simpson and published by Valley Press, an "indie" publisher that I've admired for a long time.

There's a great selection of poets and poetries on show here; a diverse mix, some newer names and some poets who could rightly claim to have been interested in some of these ideas for decades. The sequence of section headers, which move us from Emergency, to Grief, to Transformation, to Work, to Rewilding, could perhaps read like a list of the required actions or states-of-mind which we must move through in order to deal with the current state of the world.

It seems unfair to single out individual poets and poems as, even though we cannot understate the potential of a single poem, as Kate Simpson's introduction makes clear to us, the power of these poems is in their collective, eclectic response. Simpson's introduction reminds us that the word "anthology can be read as a 'bouquet' – from the Greek 'anthos' ('flower') and 'legein' ('to gather' / 'pick up')" and yet she is also very clear about what is at stake:

"These poets capture the sixth mass extinction as it rolls into view, whether quietly and loudly, in the background of a stanza, or embedded in the construction of each and every line."

> If prose is a house, poetry is a man on fire running
> quite fast through it
>
> - Anne Carson, 2016

 ANDREW McMILLAN

ONE BREATH
MARY JEAN CHAN

I have been hearing it everywhere
these days, that sudden song-burst
from the throats of the still-too
young, their world too tragic for
silence, leaving them no choice but to
grip their mothers' arms as if touch
were breath, as if no sorrow could
bear this moment when a cry
becomes the world, the song that
might cost them their lives
unraveling from their throats – rising
like a blown-bubble till it bursts,
releasing its fury into howls, yawps,
gasps – all the sounds a body makes
when it becomes its own instrument,
rehearsing all the songs it has learnt
across the centuries, forgetting how
young it still is, how long moss takes
to green, how much ripening awaits.

Image: Pawel Marcinkiewicz

JACEK GUTOROW

Jacek Gutorow was born near Opole, Poland, in 1970. He has published eight volumes of poetry, six collections of critical essays, a monograph on Wallace Stevens and a fake diary. His translations include the poetry of Wallace Stevens, John Ashbery, Charles Tomlinson, Mark Ford and Simon Armitage. He teaches American Literature at the University of Opole and edits *Explorations: A Journal of Language and Literature.*

Piotr Florczyk was born in Kraków, Poland, and moved to the United States aged sixteen. He is the author of the poetry collections *From the Annals of Kraków* (Lynx House Press, 2020), *East & West* (Lost Horse Press, 2016) and the essay collection *Los Angeles Sketchbook* (Spuyten Duyvil, 2015). His translation of Anna Świrszczyńska's *Building the Barricade* (Tavern Books, 2016) won the 2017 Harold Landon Morton Award. He lives in California.

INVISIBLE (BILINGUAL EDITION)

JACEK GUTOROW, TRANS. PIOTR FLORCZYK

ARC PUBLICATIONS | £10.99 | PBS PRICE £8.25

Invisible, by Polish poet Jacek Gutorow, translated by Piotr Florczyk, gives us mainly spare, haiku-like poems that are neither overly narrative or lyrical, but, nonetheless, skilfully observe the natural and interior world in an unsettled, open way, with a trace of humour. As Gutorow writes: "Zostawiam jedną luźną nitkę" – "I leave one loose thread" ('Loose Thread').

He alludes to Homer, Plato, Pessoa, Różewicz, and Reznikoff. However, like Objectivist verse, his inviting poems of clear observation speak "at the edge of a glance" ('Madam Cézanne'), noticing the "texture of things" ('A Fragment From Lucretius'). Some poems use a painterly shorthand of images and clipped phrases. Others are cinematic in movement. For instance, 'Rituals' starts with a zoom, widens to panoramic, and ends with a close-up of the poet in a hammock.

'Neutral Light' best suggests both Gutorow's poetics and translator Florczyk's approach of using fresh, direct language. In the kind of neutral light of a Saturday morning city walk, the poet discovers "the taste and joy of the moment".

Florczyk prefaces the collection by saying that he collaborates with Gutorow, attempting to honour his "temperament and philosophical DNA". The book places originals and translations side by side. Readers may see how Florczyk focuses even on sound features in a poem such as 'At the Pond'. Although the sounds differ in the two languages, the consonance of the original is maintained.

The English version of the postwar relocation poem 'Eastern Accent' is haunting. Yet, undoubtedly the most enormously challenging poem to translate, while staying close to the poet's poetics, rhythms, and tonalities, was the penultimate poem 'Psalm'. It covers several pages, with long chant-like lines that roll in, wave after wave, all starting with "Wysyp" ("The island"). Vignettes and remnants resist fully divulging a life remembered. Florczyk's sure result is readable, cleanly lyrical, and breath-taking.

> The island is the first word that comes to mind and
> demands elaborating, like all my latent life.

LORETTA COLLINS KLOBAH

RÓŻEWICZ: A FAREWELL

I abandon poetry without regret
As if pushing off the shore

Imagination is silent
Words lag

To walk away from poetry
Is poetry, too.

RÓŻEWICZ: POŻEGNANIE

Odchodzę od poezji bez żalu
Jakbym odbijał od brzegu

Wyobraźnia milczy
Słowa zwlekają

Odchodzenie od poezji
To też poezja

Image: Joy Mwangi

TANATSEI GAMBURA

Tanatsei Gambura is a poet and cultural practitioner. *Things I Have Forgotten Before* is her debut pamphlet published by Bad Betty Press. Her work explores the possibilities of re-memory and healing in the aftermath of individual, familial, national and collective trauma. Gambura was the runner-up in the inaugural Amsterdam Open Book Prize (2020), a Rebecca Swift Foundation Women Poets' Prize longlistee (2020), and a 2021 Writing Resident at the Library Of Africa and The African Diaspora (LOATAD) and Savannah Center for Contemporary Art (SCCA). Her poems have appeared in *Prufrock Magazine, The London Reader, New Coin Poetry Journal, Poetry London* and are forthcoming in *Best New British and Irish Poets 2021*. She is an alumna of the British Council residency, "These Images are Stories", the inaugural Obsidian Foundation Writer's Retreat, and the Writerz & Scribez Griot's Well residency.

THINGS I HAVE FORGOTTEN BEFORE

BAD BETTY PRESS | £6.00 |

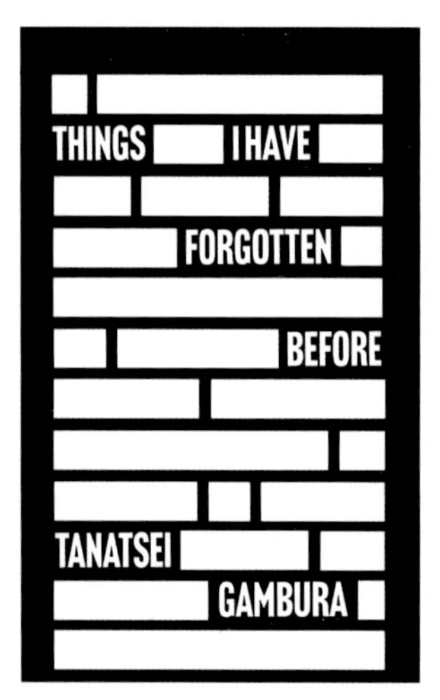

This debut pamphlet by Tanatsei Gambura is well crafted and allows the reader easy entry into hard subject matters. She walks us through the corridors of her memory which she readily admits are inaccurate guides to gain some semblance of clarity. She knows that memories hold more truth than cultural stereotypes or political propaganda. We are hitchhikers in her near present and distant past life. Gambura knows a memory is better than silence. Even when, through trauma, those memories are suppressed as a way of forgetting. Each of these poems holds their own unique form and reads like songs that bleed into each other.

> In my language, the dead are welcomed into the home.
> But the word for home is also the word for sing...
> ...Maybe home is a dirge
> invoked by dreaming, an elegy for those we can't afford to lose.

These poems are a way of holding on to the body of her people but also the body of her country. Zimbabwe to the poet is a living thing that she interrogates right down to its etymology that could be both a "large house of stone" (*dzimbadzamabwe*) or "venerated houses" (*dzimbahwe*) of chiefs.

> How do I name my child Zimbabwe without burdening them
> with a house of drystone or worrying for the lack of mortar between
> their bones?

The unspoken truth that yields across this body of work is the cost of leaving. Notice how it leaks into every sense, as demonstrated in the title poem (adjacent).

> it is august/ your visa has not arrived/ it is better to pretend
> you did not apply for one/ mama has fallen asleep/ the
> house is robed in shadows/ you do not remember when last
> there was light/ you smell of kerosene/ or gas/ or smoke
> from a fire/ you have blisters/ it is too late for harare to
> be awake/ yet your brother is not yet home/...

It will be interesting to see how this work develops into a full collection or what other spectrums of view the poet will take us on in the future. The use of craft and content are well deployed.

NICK MAKOHA & MARY JEAN CHAN

AN EXTRACT

it is august/ your visa has not arrived/ it is better to pretend you did not apply for one/ mama has fallen asleep/ the house is robed in shadows/ you do not remember when last there was light/ you smell of kerosene/ or gas/ or smoke from a fire/ you have blisters/ it is too late for harare to be awake/ yet your brother is not yet home/ he is thirteen/ he is firmer than you were at thirteen/ you check the time and check for a message/ anything could have happened in a combi between market square and the flyover/ between rothmans and southerton police/ between hlalani kuhle and your brother's stop/ he is alone//

autumn disappoints/ you walk out of the gate into a void of darkness/ searching/ still there is no light/ you are alone/ in a kaftan dress/ a safety hazard/ you must be brave for your brother/ you remind yourself why you will not have children of your own/ a distance away a vehicle draws near/ a small figure climbs out/ his back curves towards the night/ he is small against the sky/ you are small against the sky/ you walk towards him/ he sees you/ and walks quicker into a run/ neither of you say anything/ your heart swells/ maybe your hands meet/ a heartbeat/ you are somewhere in the middle of a road/ you say nothing/ and say everything/ home is a short distance away/ you think about that visa//

THREA ALMONTASER

The poetess writes to record, to hold accountability. I write to manifest Yemen in the minds of those who read my work, as a perpetual ghost that haunts the page. I often find myself considering the line by Naomi Shihab Nye, "Our own ancestry is sifted down to us through small, essential daily tasks." I attempt to populate that poetic genre of writing about both cultural differences and different cultures when it comes to the Yemeni experience. Nye's poetry lends a fresh perspective to ordinary events, people, and objects.

The local life is something I mirror in my own writing and the familial characters therein, aiming to display stories that I feel have been underrepresented in modern literature. I proudly claim my heritage by making visible the fact I'm a Yemeni writer because I've never found contemporary work written by my people, especially of this generation. It makes me sad to know a culture so rich and ancient is hidden in this way.

The fox is one of my central preoccupations in the collection. I think I'm drawn to the idea that the trickster figure troubles things out of a kind of hunger and that in some cases, you can't tell whose side they're on. I believe it's important for poets to constantly question – my book itself is written as a mode of inquiry. With this aim, I endeavoured to ask: Who am I without these hydra-headed communities? How do I subconsciously internalise the way the white gaze writes about us in the media? What perspectives do these histories of war and famine contribute to my own familial lens?

ABOUT THE POET

Threa Almontaser's debut poetry collection *The Wild Fox of Yemen* was selected by Harryette Mullen for the Walt Whitman Award from The Academy of American Poets. She is also the recipient of awards from the Civitella Ranieri Foundation in Italy, the National Endowment for the Arts and the Fulbright program. She earned an MFA from North Carolina State University.

THE WILD FOX OF YEMEN

PICADOR | £10.99 | PBS PRICE £8.25

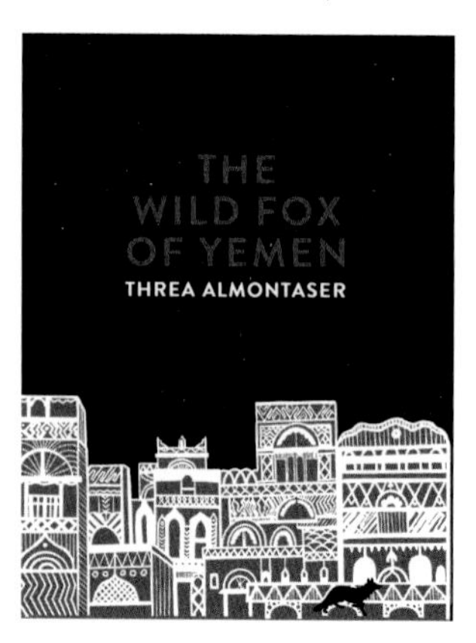

A noticeable feat in Threa Almontaser's debut collection *The Wild Fox of Yemen* is the sheer magnitude of the work. Poems which span several pages contribute to the book's overarching intention of putting the reader through what could be thought of as endurance training, a kind of extended drudgery, reflecting the experiences of the book's speakers. Driven by a torrent of complex and deft images, the poems sustain a singular freneticism, shapeshifting into sequences which seem fortified by sharp recalcitrant phrasemaking, as in the poem 'I Crack an Egg':

> A mother tasked with survival might
> miscarry the moon unnoticed.

The work appears to be very much concerned with navigating the condition and precarity of dual heritage in the U.S., along with its tendentious history and disdain for those it continues to persecute. The poem 'Portrait of this Country' opens with, "Kiss someone. God will rat on you." The implied excitement of the first clause is quickly nullified by the abrupt disappointment of what succeeds it. The use of full stops throughout the piece works to deflate the prospect of what's implied by connection and sovereignty. Speaking into the "promise of a better tomorrow" which by the mid-twentieth century had become a commonly held belief for many immigrating/migrating groups fleeing their respective countries.

Like many poems in the collection, it moves formally around the ways identities are constructed and perceived in modern day America. How notions of gender, faith, desire, and the non-white body are problematised within the white American imagination. Towards the end of the poem 'Shaytan Sneaks Bites of My Tuna Sandwich' the speaker announces, "I can't forget my mother's stories of the hidden always watching." Lines written with such lucidity and conviction carry the arguments across landscapes of memory, childhood and into the future.

Drawing on Arabic mythologies, western pop culture and current affairs, *The Wild Fox of Yemen* is a stark, bold and determined portrayal of modern American life.

ANTHONY ANAXAGOROU

AND THAT FAST, YOU'RE THINKING ABOUT THEIR BODIES

At a rooftop party, you dance near every edge. Someone drops a ring in glass, in your head the clink of a used bullet, still hot, and that fast the rooftop is covered with wires, riflemen, and you're thinking about mutiny, Mk47s, two cities clawing at each other's bruised throats while boys try to hold your hips, keep dancing. The war is on your hips. Your hands. You wear it all over. You wrap your hair in it. Pluck it from your eyebrows. The rooftop is wide and caring, too rained or sometimes incensed, and you never once think to be afraid of what could arrow a cloud and kill it. You eat volcano rolls, pink pepper goat cheese, and the war enters you. You stare at *Still Life with Flowers and Fruit* and the glade of roses scream war. Here with a doctor and your pregnant aunt who hasn't yet learned English, only speaks in war. Friends in Greensboro get picked up by bored police, get beat up for no reason, and those fists carry war. Job interviews, you carve yourself into a white-known shape and that renaming is a kind of war. You take a passport photo, told to smile without teeth, the flash a bright war. You're on the other side of mercy with your meadows and fluffed spillage, where nights are creamed with saviors. Here everyone rests on roofs graduated and sung, gazing at a sky that won't bleed them. At the beach, you're buried to the neck, practicing dead, snug in your chosen tomb, gulls flittering on all sides, waves fleshing closer, and that fast, you're thinking of a grubby desert girl who placed small stones in her scarf, shook it back and forth, said, *This is what the sea must sound like.*

AUTUMN BOOK REVIEWS

JOHN BURNSIDE: LEARNING TO SLEEP

The first poetry collection in over four years by the T.S. Eliot and Forward Prize winning poet, John Burnside. *Learning to Sleep* is haunted by the figure of Hypnos, the Greek God of Sleep, and the poet's own sleep disorder. This is an eclectic collection with innumerable characters and references from mythical icons to *The Manchurian Candidate*, the French poet Arthur Rimbaud and *Waiting for Godot*.

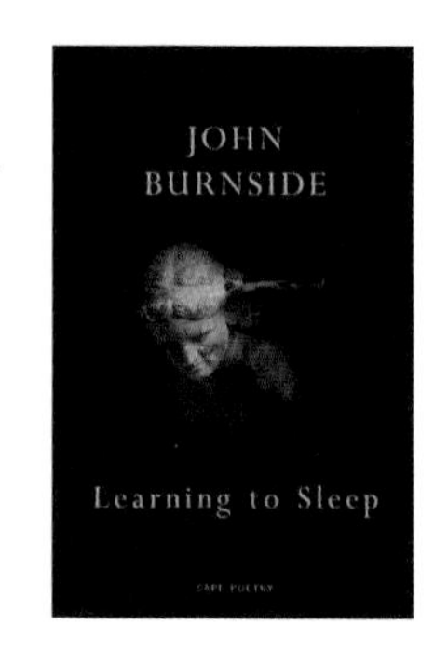

AUGUST | CAPE | £10.00 | PBS PRICE £7.50

JOHN CAREY: 100 POETS: A LITTLE ANTHOLOGY

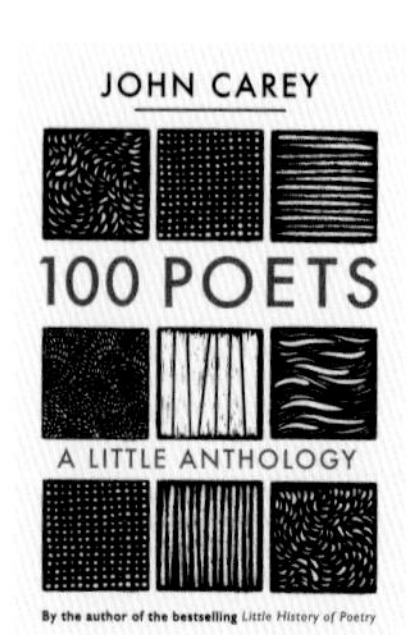

Featuring one hundred of the greatest poets from across the centuries, from Homer and Sappho to Christina Rossetti and Maya Angelou, this is a vital introduction to the very best that poetry can offer. Familiar favourites sit alongside new discoveries, each illuminated by Carey's expert commentary. This is a delightful curation of poems to treasure for a lifetime, selected by the author of *The Little History of Poetry*.

SEPT | YALE | £14.99 (HB) | PBS PRICE £11.25

BILLY COLLINS: WHALE DAY

Recent U.S. Poet Laureate Billy Collins offers a deft, colourful, and humorous new collection. *Whale Day* is elegantly conversational, slipping through topics such as the habits of a beloved dog, the attractions of Paris, and the behaviour of mice. Everyday subjects are rendered with total clarity, revealing the profundity which lies beneath, and the value of, our lived experiences.

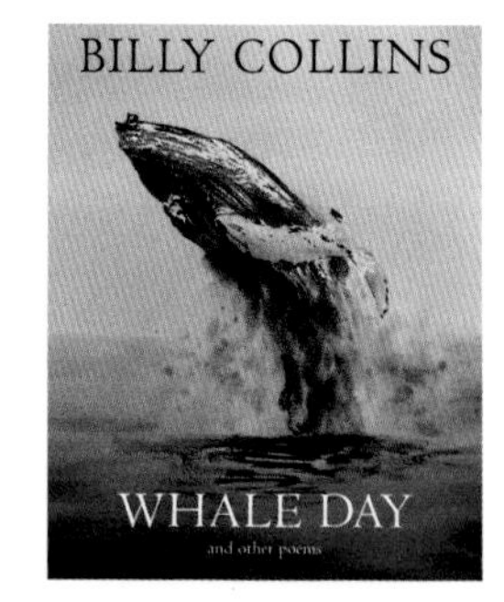

SEPTEMBER | PICADOR | £10.99 | PBS PRICE £8.25

PARWANA FAYYAZ: FORTY NAMES

In this astonishing debut the Forward prize-winning Afghan poet Parwana Fayyaz gives voice to silenced women, from her colourful ancestors to forty women hidden in mountain caves. For, in naming, she brings them back to life, "What else is there in the names and naming? / If not for reparation." At the heart of these tales is the ongoing fight for women's rights, education and her homeland: "Where do we go next? Now that our country is free."

JULY | CARCANET | £10.99 | PBS PRICE £8.25

ED. NICK HAVELY: AFTER DANTE: POETS IN PURGATORY

Released for the 700th anniversary of the great poet's death, *After Dante* is a sweeping omnibus including translations of, and poems on, Dante's *Purgatorio* by John Kinsella, A.E. Stallings, and the late Michael O'Neill. This is a fascinating testament to the inspirational power of Dante's work, and a compelling, accomplished display of translations by anglophone writers from around the world.

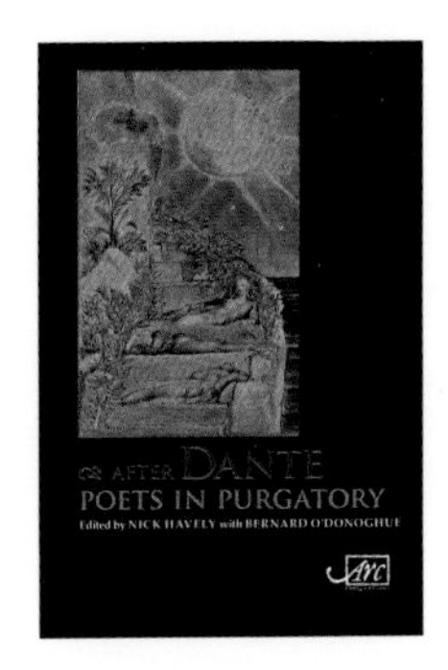

JULY | ARC | £19.99 | PBS PRICE £15.00

NICKI HEINEN: THERE MAY NOT BE A REASON WHY

Nicki Heinen's debut *There May Not Be a Reason Why* explores hospitalisation under the Mental Health Act, containing vivid descriptions of hospitals from the poet's own experience. Her work is full of imagination and intense imagery. Houseplants come to life "though not for the reason you think", choirs of monks appear on the radio and moths "whisper like whipped cream", all against the backdrop of "a pool the colour of lorazepam" and "quiet and elastic" days.

SEPT | VERVE POETRY PRESS | £9.99 | PBS PRICE £7.50

SELIMA HILL: MEN WHO FEED PIGEONS

Selima Hill's twenty-first collection contains seven sequences, which focus on different types of men and their relationships with women. Hill's poems are finely crafted, perfectly balanced between the everyday and the extraordinary. She imagines farmers, fathers, anaesthetists, dukes, and classics teachers in quick succession, all captured in her clear and perceptive voice. "Celeriac is not the same as celery; a boyfriend's not the same as an ex", she notes.

SEPTEMBER | BLOODAXE BOOKS | £12.00 | PBS PRICE £9.00

AARON KENT: ANGELS THE SIZE OF HOUSES

Aaron Kent's first full collection, *Angels the Size of Houses*, is a feat of inventive language. These poems deal with pain, illness, parenthood, grief and myth. Nothing is ever quite what you expect – a book is bought "in the art of rebellion against the dynamics of traffic management" and he writes, "You are fresh in the morning dew, and wearing / the same shapes I gave to that sweet, derelict, old / church we married in."

JULY | SHEARSMAN BOOKS | £10.95 | PBS PRICE £8.22

ABDELLATIF LAÂBI: MY MOTHER'S LANGUAGE

Renowned as one of Morocco's greatest living poets, Abdellatif Laâbi was imprisoned from 1972 to 1980 and has lived in exile in Paris since 1985. This bilingual selection of his greatest works includes the moving title poem 'My Mother's Language', translated by André Naffis-Sahely – "It's been twenty years since I last saw my mother / but I am the last man / who still speaks her language" – and an insightful afterword by Yousif M. Qasmiyeh.

JUNE | PTC | £7.00 | PBS PRICE £6.30

ED. MAISIE LAWRENCE & RISHI DASTIDAR
TOO YOUNG, TOO LOUD, TOO DIFFERENT

One Friday night in a Brixton Kitchen, Malika Booker and Roger Robinson founded Malika's Poetry Kitchen to nurture new writers from beyond the establishment. *Too Young, Too Loud, Too Different* celebrates twenty years of this remarkable collective and its extraordinary legacy. Poets from Warsan Shire to Inua Ellams cook up a storm in this feast for the senses – a fitting testament to the "Kitchen's" power to inspire generations of poets from all walks of life.

AUGUST | CORSAIR | £12.99 | PBS PRICE £9.75

GAIL McCONNELL: THE SUN IS OPEN

The Sun is Open is Gail McConnell's second collection and explores a boxed archive of public and private materials relating to the life and death of the poet's father, who was murdered by the IRA outside their Belfast home in 1984. The collection moves seamlessly between found materials, from newsprint to an account book, through past and present, all of it carefully considered to piece together a history and a life.

SEPT | PENNED IN THE MARGINS | £9.99 | PBS PRICE £7.50

KAE TEMPEST: PARADISE

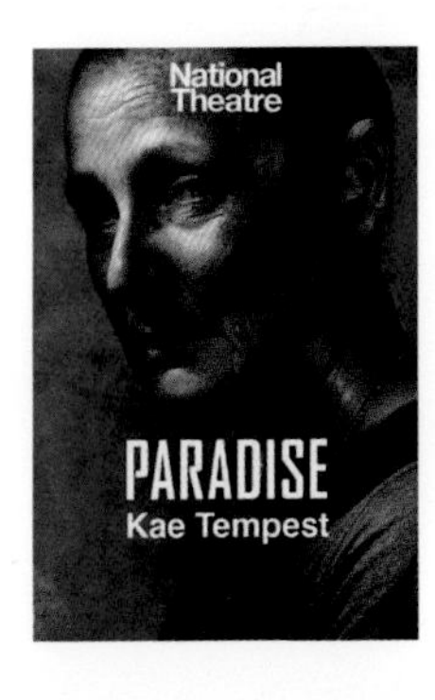

Launching at the National Theatre this Summer, *Paradise* is a dynamic reimagining of *Philoctetes* by Sophocles from Spoken Word sensation Kae Tempest. Ancient mythology leaps off the page in Tempest's quick-fire dialogue as Odysseus tries to bring the shell-shocked Philoctetes back to the Trojan War. This lyrical play re-examines "unending war", both ancient and modern, and raises urgent questions about our own "island rich with human poor".

AUGUST | PAN MCMILLAN | £10.99 | PBS PRICE £8.25

AUTUMN PAMPHLETS

GERALDINE CLARKSON: CRUCIFOX

Hailed by Kathryn Maris as "quietly, attentively, humbly – writing some of the best poems of our time", Clarkson fills this new pamphlet with rich and intricate verse. Playful and absorbing, *Crucifox* twists expectations and teeters on the surreal. Within these pages are strange relationships, visits to peculiar bookshops, monasteries and monks, and an ode to an office cleaner bundled into a unique and utterly engaging whole.

VERVE POETRY PRESS | £7.50 |

AE HEE LEE: DEAR BEAR,

Ae Hee Lee is an American poet born in South Korea. *Dear Bear,* takes the form of a mythical sequence of love letters, filled with camellias, post-glacial forests, hibernations, and transformations. "This is how my disappearance would go: my limbs would leave me first, camouflage themselves into branches, my hair would dissolve into greenery next, mime the leaves, breathe in unison." This pamphlet is an act of metamorphosis, trees vanish into black needles, and flowers cut off their roots and leap from the bush.

PLATYPUS PRESS | £7.00 |

RACHAEL MATTHEWS: DO NOT BE LULLED BY THE DAINTY STARLIKE BLOSSOM

"The daughter of circus performers and steel workers", Rachael Matthews throws each poem into the air, juggling the "family circus" of domesticity and the dark comedy of the everyday. Here are poems about desire, "our ordinary / and out of the ordinary inside love", pregnancy in a same-sex relationship, "i had miscarried my gender / so i could live in my own body", and the art of surviving early motherhood.

THE EMMA PRESS | £6.50 |

S. NIROSHINI: DARLING GIRL

Darling Girl is S. Niroshini's debut pamphlet published by Bad Betty Press. Her poems concern girlhood, history and violence. In Niroshini's work, "time has been vanquished by Uber Eats and breakfast TV", history collides with the present, as we move from Neruda's latrine, to period parties, a rooftop on Colombo, and a battlefield with the Hindu goddess Kali. Niroshini moves nimbly through her topics, with an astute and lyrical voice.

BAD BETTY PRESS | £6.00 |

GBOYEGA ODUBANJO: AUNTY UNCLE POEMS

One of the most exciting new poetry talents writing today, Gboyega Odubanjo is a British-Nigerian poet born and raised in East London, a member of the Roundhouse Poetry Collective and a Barbican Young Poet alumnus. His New Poet's Prize winning pamphlet offers a funny, thought-provoking insight into family, "all the Nigerian aunties and uncles", community and belonging. An exhilarating tour-de-force from one to watch.

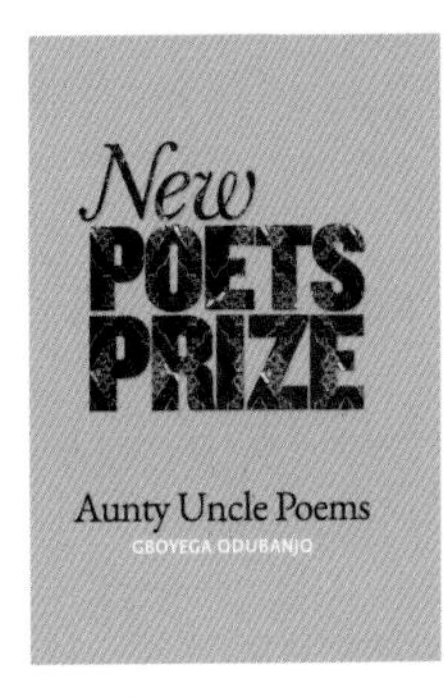

THE POETRY BUSINESS | £5.00 |

JON STONE: UNRAVELANCHE

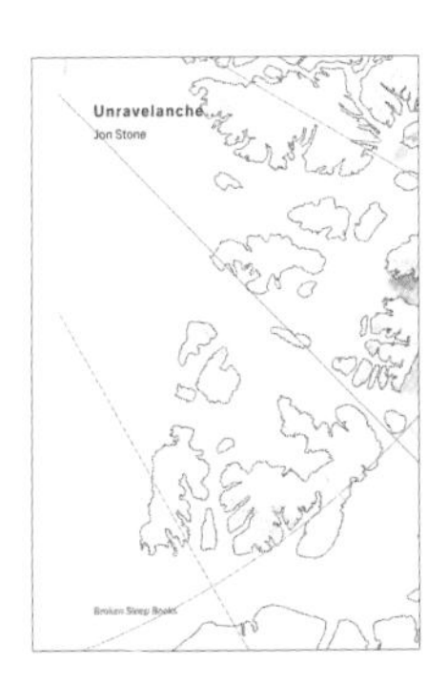

Comprised of an experimental sequence of snowstorm poems (or "snowems") in which fragments of literature are blown across the page, *Unravelanche* begins with an image of an "ice pilot" venturing out across an unpredictable arctic space. This is akin to the reader's own experience of this curious and intriguing pamphlet; never knowing what will be discovered next, deciphering meaning and imagining possibilities from the white expanse between words.

BROKEN SLEEP BOOKS | £7.00 |

AUTUMN BOOK LISTINGS

AUTHOR	TITLE	PUBLISHER	RRP
Raymond Antrobus	All the Names Given	Picador	£10.99
Sheri Benning	Field Requiem	Carcanet Press	£11.99
Linda Black	Then	Shearsman Books	£10.95
Rachel Bower	These Mothers of Gods	Fly on the Wall Press	£8.99
John Burnside	Learning to Sleep	Jonathan Cape	£10.00
Zoë Brigley & Kristian Evans	100 Poems to Save the Earth	Seren	£12.99
Miles Burrows	Take us the Little Foxes: Collected Poems	Carcanet Press	£14.99
James Caruth	Speechless at Inch	The Poetry Business	£9.95
Billy Collins	Whale Day	Picador	£10.99
Meg Cox	A Square of Sunlight	The Poetry Business	£6.50
Rishi Dastidar & Maisie Lawrence	Too Young, Too Loud, Too Different: Poems from Malika's Poetry Kitchen	Corsair	£12.99
Jaydn DeWald	The Rosebud Variations	Broken Sleep Books	£8.99
Jeremy Dixon	A Voice Coming from Then	Arachne Press	£8.99
Jane Duran	the clarity of distant things	Carcanet Press	£11.99
Adrian Earle	We Are Always and Forever Ending	Broken Sleep Books	£9.99
Maia Elsner	overrun by wild boars	flipped eye publishing	£6.95
Anthony Etherin	Slate Petals (and Other Wordscapes)	Penteract Press	£14.00
Parwana Fayyaz	Forty Names	Carcanet Press	£10.99
Angela France	Terminarchy	Nine Arches Press	£9.99
Mary Frances	Untravelling	Penteract Press	£14.00
Ed. Aaron Kent & Matt Haigh	Hit Points: An Anthology of Video Game Poetry	Broken Sleep Books	£11.99
Nicki Heinen	There May Not be a Reason Why	Verve Poetry Press	£9.99
Nazifa Islam	Forlorn Light	Shearsman Books	£10.95
Selima Hill	Men Who Feed Pigeons	Bloodaxe Books	£12.00
E.E. Jones	The Incident	Smokestack Books	£7.99
Aaron Kent	Angels the Size of Houses	Shearsman Books	£10.95
Carola Luther	On the Way to Jerusalem Farm	Carcanet Press	£11.99
Hannah Lowe	The Kids	Bloodaxe Books	£10.99
Gail McConnell	The Sun is Open	Penned in the Margins	£9.99
Afric McGlinchey	Tied to the Wind	Broken Sleep Books	£11.99
Nicky Melville	Decade of Cu ts	Blue Diode Press	£12.00
Stephanie Norgate	The Conversation	Bloodaxe Books	£10.99
Ed. Nick Havely & Bernard O'Donoghue	After Dante: Poets in Purgatory	Arc Publications	£14.99
Stephen Payne	The Windmill Proof	HappenStance Press	£10.00
Stephen Sexton	Cheryl's Destinies	Penguin Press	£9.99
Ed. Kate Simpson	Out of Time: Poetry from the Climate Emergency	Valley Press	£10.99
Daniel Sluman	single window	Nine Arches Press	£9.99
Ruth Valentine	If You Want Thunder	Smokestack Books	£7.99
Gregory Woods	Records of an Incitement to Silence	Carcanet Press	£12.99
Robert Wells	Veii and Other Poems	Carcanet Press	£10.99
Various	100 Poets: A Little Anthology	Yale University Press	£14.99

TRANSLATIONS

Milan Děžinský, trans. Nathan Fields	A Secret Life	Blue Diode Press	£10.00
Jacek Gutorow, trans. Piotr Florczyk	Invisible Bilingual Polish-English edition	Arc Publications	£7.99
Abdellatif Laâbi, trans. André Naffis-Sahely	My Mother's Language Bilingual French-English edition	Poetry Translation Centre	£7.00